I0559292

A Very High CALLING

Funny Vignettes From Years of Teaching

"The more you read
the more things you know.
The more that you learn
the more places you'll go."

Dr. Seuss

Copyright © 2024 by Nancy Miller

All rights reserved. No part of this book may be used or reproduced by any means, graphic, electronic or mechanical, including photocopying, recording, taping or by any information storage retrieval system, without the written permission of the author, except in the case of brief quotations embodied in reviews.

Title page quote from Dr. Seuss, *I Can Read With My Eyes Shut!* (New York: Random House). Copyright ©1978 by Dr. Seuss Enterprises, L.P.

*Some names in this book have been changed to protect the guilty.

Paperback ISBN 978-1-960007-62-9

Published by
Orison Publishers, Inc.
PO Box 188
Grantham, PA 17027
www.OrisonPublishers.com

A Very High
CALLING

Funny Vignettes From
Years of Teaching

NANCY COLEMAN MILLER

This book is dedicated to my parents
Ruth Mowry Miller
&
Jonathan Franklin Miller.

I thank my mother for passing on
her love of teaching to me.
I thank my dad for his gift of a sense of humor.

Contents

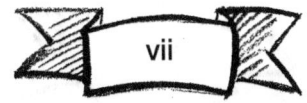

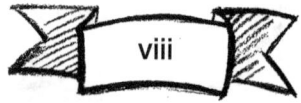

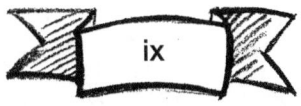

Introduction

"A Very High Calling"

I t was a hot Sunday afternoon in early August of 1965. I had just received my Master's Degree in Elementary Education from the University of Pittsburgh. My head was filled with pride knowing I had taught 100 first graders to read. It was also filled with the two unsatisfactory ratings I had received due to poor classroom management. If I were to get a third unsatisfactory rating, I would lose my teaching license forever. With all this going on in my head I knew I couldn't return to my previous job. Looking back, I realized that my management ratings were partly the result of no backup from former principals. Needing to find the perfect school was imperative. A miracle was needed.

Sitting at my desk, I found myself with a dilemma. Where would my journey take me? I wanted to teach. Suddenly I had an epiphany. It was like I was being led to something exciting. I pulled out my portable Royal typewriter

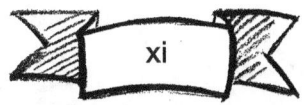

and started a letter to the Hershey Public Schools, asking if there were any teaching positions available this late in the summer. I addressed the envelope to the Superintendent of Schools, Hershey Public Schools. Why I picked this area was unknown to me at the time because all I knew about Hershey was the Milton Hershey School, Hershey Park and, of course the chocolate factory. Folding my letter into the envelope, I visualized it floating onto the proper desk. I later learned that it did find where it needed to go even though it should have been addressed to the Derry Township School District.

Taking a chance that they had received my letter. I nervously called the school on Tuesday. The Superintendent's secretary answered, informing me that they had indeed received by letter. I was given an appointment for Thursday. I would be meeting with both the Superintendent and the Director of Elementary Education.

Hoping to make a good impression, I arrived early for my appointment. I found myself facing two of the finest men I had ever known. Telling Dr. Jacques and Mr. King of my teaching journey, they were very understanding. I was excited to learn that Dr. Jacques had earned at least one of his degrees at the University of Pittsburgh. At that time, I told how I was led to Hershey. Dr. Jacques ended the interview by offering me either a fourth or a

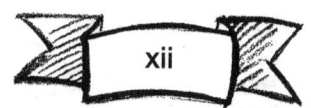

fifth-grade position. Since I had student taught in fourth grade, I chose the fifth grade. He said he would be meeting with the school board on Monday and would recommend me for the fifth-grade position.

Continuing his kindness, Mr. King and I went to his office and I was given a list of available apartments in town. "If you were my daughter Nancy," pointing to the list, "I would recommend either of these two." By the end of the day, I had rented one of them, a second-floor apartment with my own side entrance for $85.00 a month. I was on my way.

School started and, wouldn't you know, my classroom management was immediately tested. My new class had twenty-two boys and nine girls. Just getting them to the cafeteria was a major challenge. But it was fun and I loved it.

Mr. King visited my room about twice a month which was a bit unsettling at first, but I found him to be unlike the other principals I had experienced. He was kind and helpful. At the end of the day, I found a lovely typewritten letter in my mailbox praising me on a few points, and making thoughtful suggestions. All this was empowering and kind.

After thirty-one years and about one thousand wonderful fifth graders, I retired from the Derry Township School

District, with many dear colleagues and thousands of cherished memories.

Thanks to the Holy Spirit, I had been granted a third chance to do what I had been born to do.

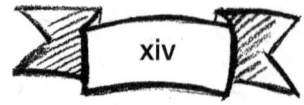

Background

I was twenty when I graduated from the University of Pittsburgh in its inaugural trimester program. I went through in two and a half years and graduated with a bachelor of Science in Education degree. I turned twenty-one in July and started teaching first grade in my hometown in September.

At my job interview, the superintendent offered me $2800 and said, "If you were a man, I would offer you $3200. Fortunately, I was living with my parents, so it was do-able.

My mother was a first-grade teacher in a rural school and I was in a school in town in the same school district. We had a wonderful time sharing experience and I learned a lot from her. Unfortunately, I was sometimes compared to her in my evaluations and was told, "You don't do this like your mother." No, I'm young and inexperienced in a school in town and she was experienced and taught in a rural school."

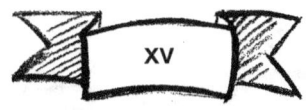

Fortunately, that never came between us. She was very sympathetic and she often said those who evaluated me came in to "snoopervise."

In the year and a half I was there, I taught about fifty darling children to read, but when I left suddenly, of my own volition, I had an unsatisfactory rating because I was challenged when it came to classroom management. I had gotten no help from my principal in that regard.

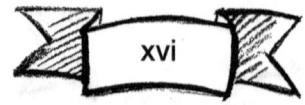

Part One
Paying it Forward

Paying it Forward #1

have had many wonderful teachers in my life, but two stand out in my memory, mainly because they have set examples of what I wanted to emulate in my teaching. A third one taught me what I did not want to emulate in my career.

In junior high, I had a wonderful young teacher for English. I also had her in senior high for Spanish. She rented a room from a neighbor and I use to watch her walk past my house on her way to school. I think I had what is referred to as a Girl Crush on her. I loved her-and still do.

In Spanish class, we had frequent vocabulary quizzes and one day, I hadn't learned my words. I suspected that we might have a quiz, so I wrote the words on the palm of my hand. During the quiz, my teacher walked quietly around the room, down the aisles. I think she must have suspected me of cheating. She walked past my desk

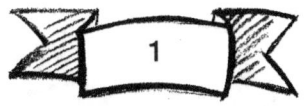

and, very quietly, slipped my paper off my desk and kept walking, never skipping a beat. I was crushed! I had never cheated before, and here I was, being caught by one of my favorite people in the world! To my knowledge, she never told anyone, not even my parents because they never said a word to me about it. They WOULD have if they had known! That experience taught me to be gentle with children who make an unwise decision.

My second experience was with a wonderful young professor of anthropology in my freshman year at the University of Pittsburgh in the spring of 1960. Our class met at 8:00 AM, three times a week in a huge lecture hall. I loved the class and never missed. He made the subject so exciting that, for a while, I wanted to be an anthropologist and go on "digs" all over the world, like he did.

In those days, we took our tests out of "blue books", in which we answered our essay questions. I always did well on that portion of his tests, but I did not do well on the objective parts of the test. I am not a good test-taker in objective tests. I love the essay parts.

In the last week of classes, he called my name and asked me to see him after class. I stopped at the podium on my way out and he asked me to go to his office with him. I had no idea what he wanted me to do.

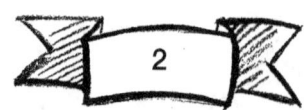

2

In his office, he asked me to sit down. He sat down behind his desk and said, "Nancy, you have never missed a class and you seem to be very attentive. I don't know why you are not doing well on the tests. You do well on the essay questions, but you have trouble with the objective questions. Explain it to me."

I told him what I have trouble with and he seemed to understand. He turned to the vast bookcase behind his desk and pulled out two paperback books. "Right now, you have a "D" average in your classwork and you are NOT a "D" student! I want you to read these two books and have a written report on each one on my desk two weeks from today. I am on my way to the dean's office to change your grade to a "C". Tomorrow, I am going to Africa on a "dig" and will be back in two weeks. You have your "C". You don't HAVE to do what I ask, but if you don't, don't ever let me see you on campus."

I went back to my dorm, read the two books – I loved them, and wrote reports on them. They were on his desk when he returned from his "dig."

I saw him many times on campus and we always greeted each other. I thanked him every time we met. This wonderful teacher taught me to always see the student as a real person, give him/her a chance to redeem the situation and to honor the student's abilities.

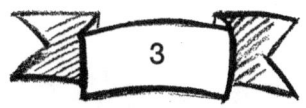

Paying It Forward #2

I was a sophomore at the University of Pittsburgh in the spring of 1961. I had been accepted into the School of Education. At Pitt, every student had to take four semesters of Liberal Arts before specializing in a given field of study. I was in a Geography class which was taught by an adjunct professor from the southwest.

We were given the assignment of a research paper about some aspect of geography. I love libraries and research, so I got to work. It was just before any online research and long before the Google method of research. I had access to the wonderful Pitt Library and the public Carnegie Library on the border of our large campus.

I decided to find out all I could about a sand quarry on the south mountain in Cumberland County (my home county.) As a family, we could always see it on our way to our summer cottage at a nearby State Park. I got to work

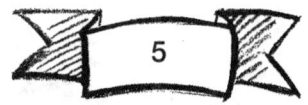

loving every minute of it. I had a green portable Royal type-writer and about one hundred 3x5 index cards. That's how research was done in those days. All of this, while I carried fifteen other credits!

About two weeks later, I submitted my paper, complete with charts and graphs. I had a great feeling of accomplishment.

When I went to class a few days after handing it in, my professor announced before the end of class that he wanted to talk with me after class. I met him at his podium.

"Whose Master's Thesis did you plagiarize?"

"No one's. I wrote that paper."

"Do you have notecards in your writing?"

"Yes, but they're back at the dorm. I can get them."

"First, I want you to write your name on this paper. If you did indeed write this paper, you have an A in the course. Meet me in my office in thirty minutes. I am on the sixth floor of the Cathedral, number 636."

I raced across the street to my dorm and returned with my stack of about one hundred index cards in my own

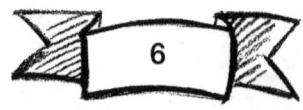

handwriting. I went back across the street and met him in his office. He looked through them and nodded his head in a conciliatory nod. I thought I had won.

"Where did you do you research?"

"Some of it here in our library, but most of it at Carnegie."

"Let's go."

"I have a class in an hour."

"Let's go."

We walked across the campus, not saying anything.

We entered the Science Room of the Carnegie. The librarian looked up from her work and said, "I thought you were finished with your paper."

"I am, but this man doesn't believe that I wrote it." She shook her head and threw her hands in the air.

"This girl has spent hours here doing research on some sand quarry out east. I know she wrote that paper."

I got a B in the course.

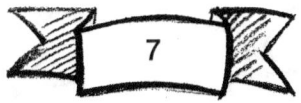

Needless to say, I learned a very important lesson for my career. I always talked with a child about an issue and, with the help of other professionals, if necessary, we would resolve the problem.

Addendum

I will always remember the two wonderful teachers by name, but I call this man Joe the Jerk because I don't remember his name, but he taught me a valuable lesson.

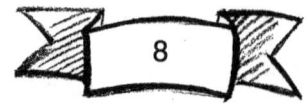

Part Two

Stories

Doug and Tommy

About ten of my first graders were in a reading circle and the others were back at their desks doing their morning's work. We were reading and discussing what we had just read.

Doug and Tommy were best friends and they were sitting next to each other in the circle. Doug was the youngest in a family of four boys. Tommy was the only boy in a family with two girls.

Tommy noticed that Doug's fly was open and he quietly nudged him. "Your barn door is open. The horse will get out."

"It can't get out if it can't get up!"

It took all my control not to laugh out loud.

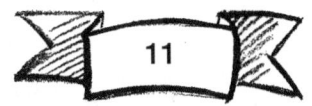

Joey

I was fresh out of college, teaching first grade in my hometown. I had about 25 children and was teaching a reading curriculum called Phonetic Keys to Reading. It was wonderful for the children. We had words at the bottom of the page which illustrated the letter or rule for the day… "When two vowels go walking, the first one does the talking and the second is silent." The children would draw a line over the first vowel and cross out the second. Above the line of words were pictures and words telling the names of the pictures, i.e. bike, knife, and pie, illustrating the "long I" rule. The boys really like it because it was somewhat mechanical.

A little guy named Joey was always attentive and did what he was supposed to do in his book.

The day the children returned to school after Christmas vacation, Joey announced to me, "I'm going to learn to read today." And he did! Something had clicked in over the

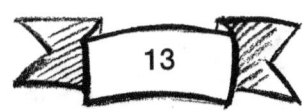

Holidays and he read very well from then on. He became an avid reader through the Spring.

One day at the school library, he was curled up in a corner of the room where the fourth-grade books were located. Strange as it may seem now, our children were to select and read books only from their own grade level section. I looked across the room and saw Joey with a fourth-grade science book perched on his knees.

I walked over to him and he said, "I'm having trouble with this one word. I think it is chemistry." (with the sound of "ch" as in "church.")

I said, "Oh, Honey, sometimes "ch" can also say a "k" sound. Try it that way. We would put it in jail for not following the rule."

He did and his face lit up as only a young child's face can when he has an "aha" moment.

"Oh, "k"emistry! My big brother has that in high school!"

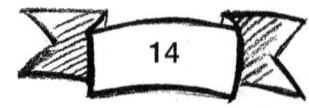

Sammy

My first three years of teaching reading in first grade. I loved it while I did it, but after I went to fifth grade, I would have never wanted to go back to first.

It was a typical day in my first-grade classroom back in the 60's with three reading groups; the Robins, the Bluejays and the Cardinals. I had called the Robins up to the reading circle for their daily lesson and the Bluejays and the Cardinals were in their seats, doing their seatwork.

I looked up and there was a bit of a commotion in the back of the room. Sammy was going to the cloakroom and I asked him where he was going and he said, "Home."

"No, you need to work on your seatwork until I call your group up front," I said. He returned to his seat with a sheepish expression on his little face.

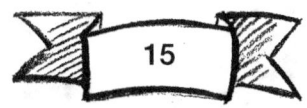

A few minutes later, I looked up, and the same thing was happening again. This time, I got up and went back to him. I put my hand on his shoulder and bent down and said, "Sammy, you must return to your seat and finish your work." He looked like he was going to cry so I gave him a little hug and he returned to his seat rather reluctantly.

As I was dismissing the Robins from their lesson, Sammy was out of his seat again.

As I approached him, I saw that he was close to tears. I gave him a hug and asked him, "Honey, what's the matter?"

He looked at me and "Well, I'll tell you. I've had about as much of this as I can take."

I had to suppress a laugh at his answer. I talked quietly with him and calmed him down. I called his group up to reading circle and he was okay. I had told him that we'd go out to recess after his group lesson. He seemed happy with that.

"The Tiger Walks"

I was teaching first grade in a large inner-city school in Pittsburgh in the mid-60's. My principal left a lot to be desired when it came to teacher support. Our elementary supervisor was in the same category. They did not like each other and had opposite "teaching styles" for their teachers, long before teaching styles were something to be taken into consideration when it came to teaching children or evaluating teachers. This made it very difficult in a school which already had many problems for students and for teachers. Fortunately, we teachers were well aware of this issue and we secretly "stuck together."

Those of us in the primary grades were located on the first floor and the intermediate grades were on the second floor. Most of the time, we taught our children in our principal's mode, but when the elementary supervisor was on-site, a note quickly passed from room-to-room

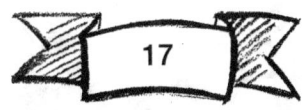

stating that "The Tiger Walks." We teachers, in self-defense, would switch to the Tiger's style. Wonderful for the children?

Jamal

Jamal was a darling little boy in my inner-city first grade back in the sixties. We were studying about nature and what a farmer or gardener uses in creating a garden. I had a shovel and other gardening tools. The children were gathered around in a circle at my feet. I was showing them the different tools and telling how and why they are used. As I held up a hoe and showed how it helped the person using it, Jamal said, "My sister be a hoe, but she don't look nothin' like that." It was all I could do not to burst out laughing, but I controlled myself in an effort no to hurt his feelings.

Rules of Room 62

For most of my time in fifth grade, some of the other teachers spent a considerable bit of time on the first day helping the children create a list of rules for their room. This list could stretch from the base of the cursive Peterson Penmanship alphabet strip above the blackboard to the very edge of the chalk tray at the bottom. I've even seen a second "layer" with the same borders. Not in Room 62!

Our room was not a democracy. I made the rules and the children understood them and followed them. They were The Golden Rule and Do Your Homework. We did spend some time discussing them. I always ended the discussion with, "I say what I mean and I mean what I say."

At the end of September at Back-to-School night, I shared the rules with parents and they always seemed to approve. I also told them, "I will help you raise your child if you let

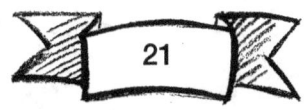

me." They liked that and it was long before the expression, "It takes a village."

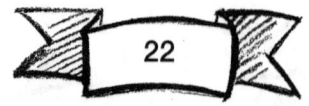

Report Card

Our children got their report cards every nine weeks – 4 times a year We had a very simple grading scale:

    90-100 – A
    80-90 – B
    70-80 – C etc.

Before I gave my homeroom children their cards, I would say, "I did not give you any grade. I simply recorded what you have earned. If you earned and 88 or 89, according to the 60-70 grades I had for you in my grade book, - you might get an A or a B – depending on your attitude or co-operation in class. In any case I recorded what you earned.

The children understood this very well. I never had a problem of any kind.

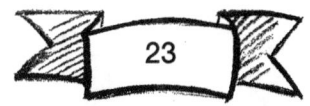

Prepositions

My room was the largest classroom in a very large building. We had twelve or thirteen sections of every grade K-5. Every year in the late fall, I would write a long sentence on the board that stretched from one side of the room to the other. It was the day I introduced my fifth graders to prepositions. "On Sunday, before church, I drove in my car to the store on the corner for bread, for dinner, in the rain."

I told the children that the subject and the predicate can never be in a prepositional phrase, at which time I drew parentheses around all the prepositional phrases. That left "I went." The children laughed.

I proceeded to write about 45 prepositions on the board in alphabetical order and they wrote them on paper. One of the boys raised his hand and asked me why I didn't just give them a list on paper. I said, "Because there is a connection between

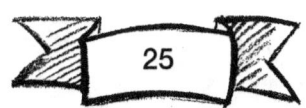

your hand and your brain. You will know a lot of them by the time you're done writing them for yourself. By next Monday, each of you will stand up front and say them in order. Now, no one will ever stop you on Chocolate Avenue and ask you to say them, but you will learn the very important skill of memorizing in the process." After a bit of moaning, I told them how to "chunk" them. "Take the A's, B's D's and F's tonight, then add more tomorrow night and so on. We'll practice them every day for a few minutes." By Wednesday or Thursday, most of the kids had mastered the whole list. On Friday a few of them asked if they could say them that day. Of course, I said yes, with a wonderful feeling inside my best teacher-self.

Years later, my students would stop in to see me and tell me that their high school English teachers would say, "I'll bet you had Miss Miller in fifth grade English. Your sentence structure is excellent."

The crowning glory of this story is that years later, long after I had retired, a young waitress gave me a big hug as she seated us at her table and said, "Miss Miller, I can still say my prepositions in alphabetical order!" As she proceeded to rattle them off, my friends at the table looked at her in utter amazement and clapped when she was done. I could have cried! It was a lesson in self-discipline and self-confidence for the children and I had given them the lifelong skill of memorizing important information.

Danny

Danny was a sweet, quiet child and he had many friends in my class. He left the room for a speech therapy check-up occasionally. He was in the monitoring stage and just needed to report to our speech clinician for a periodical check-in. Our clinician was a beautiful, kind woman who loved the children. She was also very stylish.

One day, at recess, another child was teasing him about have to do this. I overheard him say, with his hands on his hips, "Look, if you have a problem with my going to her, it's your problem, not mine." He walked away, very happy with himself.

I thought, "Good job, Danny!"

Years later, I answered my doorbell, and there stood Danny, in his USPS uniform and his heavy mailbag over

his shoulder. "I just wanted to check if you were the same Nancy Miller as my fifth-grade teacher." We recalled the incident and had a good laugh. I told him how proud I was of him.

Patrick

Patrick was the only child of an older couple and he was accustomed to getting his own way. He was a nice boy, but when things didn't go his way, his stubborn streak came into play.

He had an uncanny way of looking busy when he really wasn't. We were working on our Helen Keller Project – a very intensive research project in which the children worked at their own pace for an hour and a half a day. I conferenced with each child weekly and helped them set their individual goals for the next week. When I talked with Patrick, it became obvious the he hadn't met his goals for the week because he hadn't worked very hard.

Our class was to take a day-long field trip to Philadelphia the next day and we were all very excited about it. In our conference, I told Patrick that he had to take his project home that night and we set a reasonable goal for homework

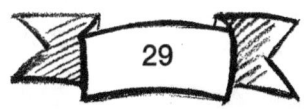

which he could easily do in about an hour. He also had to write his parents a note telling them the situation. I approved his note, which said that unless he accomplished his night's goal and had his parents sign the note, he would not be going on the field trip.

I was very surprised and disappointed the next morning when Patrick appeared at school without his work done and without his note. I took him aside and asked him why. I thought maybe there was a problem at home, but he just shrugged his shoulders and said, "I just didn't feel like doing it." I suspected that maybe there was a serious problem at home so I called and his mother assured me that everything was okay at home. I told her the situation and she got angry at me.

I gave Patrick a day's worth of work, including his project and sent him next door to my friend. We had thirteen fifth grades in one hall and we supported each other in such situations. We went to Philadelphia without him.

The next day, the mother, Patrick and I had a meeting with the principal and she was angry at me to start with, but she was embarrassed and angry at Patrick when she left.

Many years later, I saw his mother at the grocery store and asked her about Patrick. She got a sheepish look on her

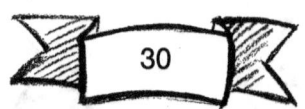

face and said, "You tried to alert us twenty-five years ago. He is working part time, living at home, and driving us crazy."

I felt sorry for her, but, as I used to say at Back-to-School Night, "I will help you raise your child if you let me."

Field Day

F or all of my years of teaching in Hershey, our elementary school was very large. We had sixty-eight classrooms for grades kindergarten through fifth grade. There were twelve or thirteen classes of each grade which was wonderful. The primary grades were self-contained, but most of the intermediate classes were taught departmentally. This allowed us to teach what we loved and avoid what we didn't like. I loved the language arts and did not like math and science. Our homerooms were heterogeneous, but our subject classes were mostly homogeneous. Some years, we had one other team member and other years, we taught across the whole spectrum of the twelve or thirteen of us. I preferred just having one teammate, but both ways worked over the years.

Every spring, we spent a day outside on our high school's athletic field, having fun competing in all kinds of events. My class that year was woefully unathletic, which was fine

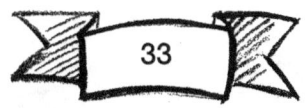

with me. Athleticism was never my strong suit and, as a kid, I dreaded gym class.

In preparation for that day, I talked with my children and told them that I wanted them to do their best, but that I'd love them, no matter the results of our day outside.

That day, we all brought a picnic lunch and went out to play. The children participated in all kinds of events, with the thirteen of us as monitors of the events. The children who were not in a given event sat or stood in class groups on the hillside and cheered for their homeroom.

It became evident early in the contest that our home-room was not doing well. The children were not discouraged and cheered as loudly as all the other groups.

At the end of our day, my children listened to the day's results. We came in last. We stood proudly on the hillside and cheered loud and class, "WE ARE NUM-BER THIRTEEN!!!

Dana

Over the thirty-one years of teaching fifth grade language arts, I was fortunate to have collected twenty-one sets of readers. That afforded me the opportunity to form small units, using stories from the various sets. We read sports stories during the World Series and, after my visiting Nigeria in 1989, we studied stories about Africa, including stories about Albert Schweitzer.

One day, during our study of Africa, I told the story about my being in an open market in the city of Lagos. As the eight of us in my party walked through the narrow walkways of the market, I noticed that the men tending their produce were sitting in a strange position. Their feet were flat on the ground, but their bottoms were about eight inches off the ground. They looked very comfortable, but I didn't know how that could be.

When the children were ready to read their story to themselves, a child asked if they could sit that way to read. Out of character for me, I said they could until it wasn't comfortable. Then they should sit back in their chair.

As I watched the children, they popped up at different times, but they didn't last very long. At the end of the story, Dana was still in that position. When she was finished, she took her seat.

We discussed the story and when we were ready to move on, I asked the children why they thought Dana was able to sit like that for the entire time.

"Because she's Jewish." I was totally taken by surprise.

"No. It's because she is a serious ice skater. While you are still asleep, she is in the Hershey Arena very early a few mornings a week skating. The muscles and the tendons in her legs and knees are stretched a lot more than yours and mine."

Rhoda

n the Eighties and Nineties, when we were still permitted to do so, I had my fifth graders memorize "Twas the Night Before Christmas." They had about two weeks to learn it. Each child had to say it alone. I taught them the importance of memorization and how to do it. We had fun with it.

Rhoda was in my class and she was Jewish. Her mother wrote me a note, asking me if her child had to do it. I said she didn't have to, but I thought it was a wonderful opportunity for her child to share some of her culture. I told her she and Rhoda could select something from the Jewish tradition which would be equal to what the others had to learn.

They chose not to do that, so Rhoda did the assignment and she did it well.

The last week of school before Christmas break, our fifth graders entertained the primary children at a Christmas

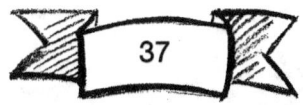

assembly in the auditorium. Prior to that event, I gave the children the opportunity to be a part of that event. I said they'd have to give up a recess to learn some simple motions. Also, if they had a Santa hat or a red or green top, they should wear it on that day. Guess who showed up in full regalia – Rhoda!

Children want to belong and she certainly proved that!

Matt

always had a soft spot in my heart for big boys. My younger brother was always big for his age and people who didn't know him expected him to act older than he was. Matt was a big boy and he was a challenge, but I loved him. He was funny and a lot of fun.

One day on the way to lunch, he and his friend Sam were acting up. I had warned them twice to stop. The third time I turned around, they were still doing it. I told them I would meet them back at the room after lunch. They were not to go to recess. As I look back now, I should have taken them back to the room and handled it right then.

After lunch, I returned to the room and had a talk with them. We agreed that they had disobeyed and deserved to be paddled. It wasn't Matt's first, but it was a first for the other child. I followed the procedure and sent them off for a drink and sent them out for recess.

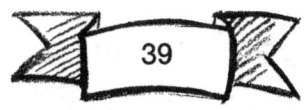

All afternoon, Sam just sat and glared at me, but Matt was his normal self. At the end of the day, I asked Matt to stay for a few minutes after all the others had gone home. He was a walker and lived across the street from our school. He stayed and I said to him, "Matt, I want to thank you for being a real gentleman this afternoon." He shrugged his shoulders and turned his head to the side. With a sheepish grin, he said, "Oh, that's okay."

The next afternoon, he asked if he could stay and talk to me. I said, "Of course, Honey."

When all the children were gone, he said, "I want to thank you for what you did yesterday."

"What was that?"

"You spanked me. I really needed that. It got rid of a lot of junk in my head. My parents couldn't figure why I was so good at home last night. I wasn't about to tell them that I had gotten spanked at school"

We had a good laugh and a big hug!

Years later, Sam was in college with the child of a family member and when she learned that he was from Hershey she asked him if he knew me. He told her that I was one of his favorite teachers!

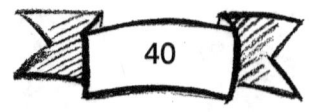

Update on Matt

I n about 2021, I was in Hershey for lunch with some of my teacher friends. I said to Jessie, Matt's parents' neighbor, "Do you ever see Matt when he's home?" I'd love to see him!" "Yes, I'll tell his parents you'd like to see him the next time he's home."

"Thanks so much! I'd love it."

A few months later I had a call from Matt. We made a date for lunch.

I drove over to Hershey and we met, but the restaurant was so full that we went over to his home for our visit.

We had such fun telling funny stories and catching up with each other's lives. His folks were there, we ate lunch, but we didn't talk about my spanking him – even forty-some years later! Before I left, we went to see my retired principal, Claude. We had a nice visit with him and his

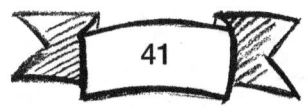

wife. When we parted, I got a big hug and he said, "You were my favorite teacher ever."

This from a 52-year-old, good-looking hulk of a Marine!

I still hear from him at Christmas!

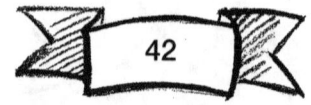

Snowflakes and Archie

I had the good fortune to teach with eleven or twelve other fifth grade teachers. We were good friends and had lots of fun together – alone or with our kids.

We gathered each morning at about 7:45 for coffee in the teachers' room. During the 70's, when "All in the Family" was very popular on TV, we would have so much fun talking about the latest episode! John, one of our teachers, pretended he was Archie! He was perfect for the part! What fun! We got loud! We often said that if our kids were that loud in the cafeteria, we'd "kill them!"

One year, about a week before Christmas, we had our children make 81/2 x11 inch snowflakes. On the last afternoon, after the kids had gone home, we got together with all their snowflakes, had a fun pot-luck

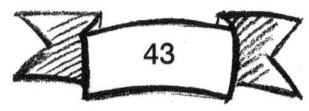

supper and hung the snowflakes from the ceiling in our two long hallways!

The place went crazy on the morning when the kids returned in the new year! They were so excited!

Sadly, it lasted only a few days. We had to take them down because they "created a fire hazard." It was fun while it lasted.

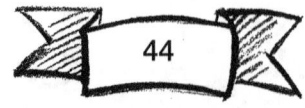

Dan

Years ago, long before we knew much about children with learning disabilities, let alone what to do about them, Dan was in my fifth-grade class. He was a big boy and was very well-behaved. His mother and I were friends and we knew that there was a problem, but we didn't have a name for it. In social studies, I required the children to learn their states and capitals and to spell them correctly.

They learned them a few at a time as we studied regions of the United States. One night my friend, Dan's mother, called me and asked, "Nancy, could I come in and take the test for Dan tomorrow? We have spent so much time over the weekend and he can name them perfectly, but can't spell them." I told her not to worry. I would test the kids the next day and he should just do the best that he can. He took the test and did know them perfectly, but couldn't spell them. I gave him full credit and sent him

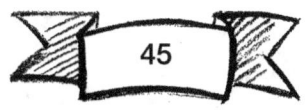

to the office on an errand while I talked with the children and explained the issue. They were fine with his getting full credit for his valiant effort.

About three years later, the family moved to Ohio and we kept in touch. That summer, a friend and I visited them in their new home. Both parents went to work one morning and Mary and I took Dan and his younger sister shopping. We stopped for lunch and the sandwich board outside the restaurant read, "Quiche and a beverage…$5.00" Dan read it is "Quickie and a beverage…$5.00" Mary and I had a quiet chuckle.

At dinner, that evening, we were telling our friends about our day, and I told Dan's parents about Dan's funny error. His dad said, "Dan, anytime you can get a beverage and a quickie for $5.00, you'd better take it." He explained what he meant and we all had a good laugh, including Dan.

Walter Concrete

Years ago, part of our fifth-grade English curriculum included newspaper reporting. This taught the children the "who, how, when, and where" of paragraph development.

Each child got up and read a fairly typical report of an imaginary or real event which had taken place in our town. The one that still stands in my mind, after all these years, is the clever child who stood up and prefaced his remarks with the introduction, "Good afternoon. This is your favorite sidewalk reporter, Walter Concrete."

Shawn

Shawn was a tall, good-looking boy in fifth grade. He walked tall and was sweet and well-behaved. In our classroom, we had a big chart on the wall with the children's spelling test record. If a child made a 100% on either the Wednesday test or the Friday test six weeks in a row, he could choose a book from the Arrow Book Box on the window sill. Shawn was one test away from choosing his book. I corrected his Friday test and he missed one word. It broke my heart to mark it wrong, but I had to.

Shawn walked back into our room from his math/science class. I had placed all the tests face-down on the children's desks. He flipped his paper over, expecting to see a 100% grade on the top, but it was a 95% instead. I had watched him do this and wasn't surprised to see him start to cry. A fifth-grade boy crying was never an issue for me, but I was a bit taken aback. I walked over to him and put my arm around his shoulder.

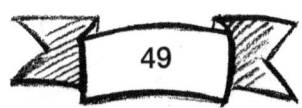

"Are you okay, Honey?'

"Yes" he sniffed.

"Come with me," I said.

I took him into a small room beside mine and said to him, "What's going on, Honey?"

He started to really cry and said, "My Grandma lives with us and she's dying." I knew his mother was a nurse and that his grandma lived with his family.

"Oh, Sweetie, what can I do for you?"

"I need a hug." Of course, I held him while he cried and talked with him. When he was cried out, I told him to go get a drink and wash his face. "Go for a walk inside the building and come back to the room when you're ready."

He returned about ten minutes later and went on with his day. At the end of the day, he came to my desk and thanked me. "You really helped me today. Thank you."

Aaron

aron was a small boy who had had spina bifida at birth and walked with Canadian crutches. He was paralyzed from the waist down. In the early to mid-seventies, there was a national appeal for fundraisers to provide for the refurbishing of the Statue of Liberty in time for our nation's Bi-centennial. Our school joined the troops and conducted a fundraiser for that purpose. Aaron solicited family and friends and raised money for walk around our school's track. He was the only child in my room who did this. On the day of the walk Aaron circumvented the long track a number of times to raise his money and honor his pledges.

His story became one of my Hero Tales in my Helen Keller Project as an example of what a handicap person can do.

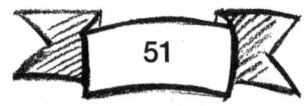

StaRR

She came to Hershey in fifth grade from Chicago. She was a tall, beautiful African-American girl who was street-smart in a nice way. She knew how to take care of herself in most situations. Her habit of silently "jivin" in her seat was distracting to me and the other children. By Christmas, I had let her know (with a look) that it was not appropriate in the classroom. She complied easily.

That spring, I had major surgery and was out of school for about six weeks. My wonderful district paid my substitute to come into school for three mornings before I left so that she could get comfortable with my Helen Keller Project. Consistency was vital for the children. She was tall and was a big woman like me, with dark hair. We could have been sisters.

I returned after my surgery and Mrs. Smith was there for two mornings to assure consistency with the Project for

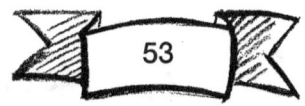

the children. It all went very smoothly. After about a week I noticed that Starr was "jivin" again. I took her out into the hall to talk with her.

"Starr, you know that you're not to do that."

"Mrs. Smith let me do it."

"I put my hands on my hips and said, "Do I look like Mrs. Smith?"

"Yes, as a matter of fact you do!"

She had me! I laughed and sent her back into the room with a friendly swat on her behind. She never "jived" again in my room.

Polar Bears

n the old days, we were permitted to decorate our rooms and hallway bulletin boards appropriately for the holidays. We had Christmas trees, Nativity scenes, and winter scenes all over the school.

In December, I decorated my hallway bulletin board with a secular Christmas scene on a totally white background. Before we left for the Christmas holiday, I removed everything but the pristine white background. I posted a sign which read "How many polar bears do you see?"

The children would stand in front of it and debate with each other about the funny question.

Teaching was SO MUCH FUN!!!

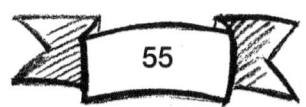

Rain, Rain, Go Away

I t was the last week of school and it had rained every day. Everyone was hoping for a nice day so that our twelve fifth grades could enjoy a fun day of competing outside in our annual field day. There was a good chance that, by afternoon, the rain would end and we could be outside.

As was my morning delight, I was standing in my doorway, greeting my children. Toward the end of the "parade", a child looked over his left shoulder and said to his friend, "You know, I've about had the shits of this weather."

He turned around and saw me, with a shocked look on his face – one of fear and dread. I just put my hands on his shoulder and said, "I totally agree."

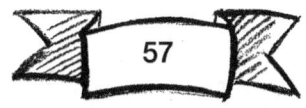

Ellen

One spring day, I was getting the children lined up to go to gym class. One little girl did not come to line. I said, "Come on, Honey."

She was close to tears and said, "I can't."

"Okay. Stay here. I'll be right back."

By the time I got back a few minutes later, she was in tears.

I walked over to her, bent down and put my arm around her. "What's the matter, Honey?"

"I don't know. I have blood on my legs."

"Are you sick at your stomach?"

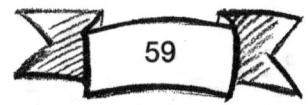

"No." She was pale and frightened.

I wrapped her jacket around her waist and we walked up to the nurse's office, hand in hand. Of course, I knew what had happened, but I was surprised. I'd had other girls who had gotten their period in fifth grade, but Ellen was such a small child. I would never have guessed that she would have been one of them.

The nurse explained to her what was happening and Ellen clung to me in disbelief. A few minutes later, her mother arrived with a change of clothes and took her home for the day.

Chuck

Chuck was a tall boy for his ten years and he sort of "ambled" when he walked. He had a droll sense of humor and he spoke with a slow drawl. He had an unusual interest in the Civil War, which was evidenced by his large collection of Civil War memorabilia. When we were studying the Civil War, he brought a lot of it to school.

One day, he came lumbering into the room with his arms full of all sorts of thing-among which was his great-grandfather's musket. Imagine! He had brought it on the school bus-back in the mid-seventies!

With a loud sigh of relief, he plopped everything on my desk-then got a scared look on his face.

"Oh, my gawd! I forgot my gym suit!"

We had a good laugh and I sent him to the office to call

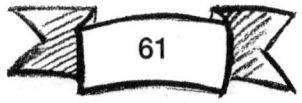

his mother. She brought his gym suit to school and he was ready to go on with his day.

Years later, he served as the Chief of Police in a nearby town.

Troy

Achild's reputation often precedes him/her into the next grade. I never liked to read about a child before the school year started. I wanted to take my chances in handling any situation. This was long before we had a lot of children with special needs, of which a teacher had to be aware ahead of time.

In the mid-eighties, Troy entered my room and it was obvious that he was going to be a challenge. He was naughty, but I liked him. I love a challenge.

At our September Back-to-School Night, I always told the parents that I would help them raise their child if they'd let me.

In those days. Pennsylvania had a law called "In Loco Parentis", which was "In Place of the Parent." This meant that a teacher or principal could mete out punishment

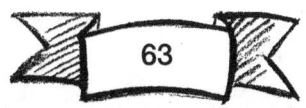

appropriate for the offense committed. In those days, that included a spanking according to strict rules.

My school's rules dictated that we take the child out into the hall, get a teacher witness, and give three swats with a small paddle. We were then to give the child time to collect himself and re-enter the classroom.

My classroom had two rules: the Golden Rule and "Do Your Homework." Break either one and "Meet me in the hall."

I would get my friend next door as a witness. We did it for each other if necessary. I always talked with the child in the hall and tell him/her why this was necessary. I'd do what I had to do – never in anger, bend down, put my arms around his/her shoulder and say, "I love you. Go get a drink take a walk around the inside of the building and come back when you're ready."

One day, all of this happened in order and I took Troy out into the hall. Everything happened as usual, and, before he left us, he got us in a group hug, and, with a tear-stained face, said, "I love you so much."

He got to take a walk to collect himself, and my friend said, "I can't do this." My witness-friend and I had to go back to our rooms and act like nothing had happened – with lumps in our throats.

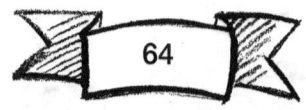

BRad

Brad came to my fifth grade from England. He was a sweet child and he spoke with a very British accent. He was well-liked by the other children.

My fifth-grade language arts class did an eighteen-week intensive research project based on the life of Helen Keller. It was a project on Handicap-Awareness. We lived in a town where the Penn State Hershey Medical Center is located and I wanted to teach the children to be kind to and tolerant of people with handicaps-temporary or permanent. We worked every day for ninety minutes for a whole semester on the project. It comprised the child's reading and English grade for two marking periods. Each child worked at his/ her own rate and I conferenced every week with each child. We set new goals for the coming week and discussed how the child achieved last week's goals and maybe why he/she hadn't. Maybe absence or interest in a different "station" was the reason. There was never any judgment implied-as long as the child understood the situation.

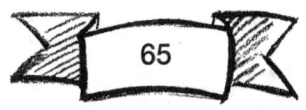

We talked early in the project about Brad's knowing different spellings for words like honour and colour and that I would be grading his papers, taking that into account. The children had no problem with that.

Built into the project was the child's learning to be organized over a long time. Each child's project folder had at least fifty papers in it at the end. Record-keeping was also important. As the child would finish a station, he/she was to check it off on a checklist, and record the score on each paper. The score was graded from minus zero which was an Excellent paper - no errors - to the number of errors on the paper. On the last day of the project, each child tallied all of his/her scores on a special paper. For each perfect paper, the worst score could be crossed off. The paper had to still be in the project folder, but the score could be neatly crossed off on the special paper. To everyone's surprise, Brad had more perfect papers than he had any with errors.

When the children were out at recess that morning, Brad was jokingly trying to "sell" his perfect scores to the other children. I took him aside and we talked about it. He said, with a chuckle, "Well, you can't blame a bloke for trying." We had a good laugh and he took his project home with a wide grin on his cute face.

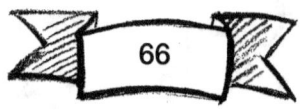

Yes and No

One of the major emphases of my wonderful Helen Keller Project was to teach the children proper respect for and empathy for people with handicaps or major health Issues. We lived in a community which was the home of the Penn State Milton S. Hershey Medical Center and Medical School. Chances were that they would encounter many people in town with major medical and mobility challenges when they were out and about in town.

One of the highlights of our study was a guest appearance of Sophie, a wonderful older blind lady and her dog guide Cody. She talked with the children and was open to any questions they had. At the end of her visit, she told them that they should never go up to a service dog and pet it without asking permission first. She told them that the dog is working and shouldn't be distracted.

She said, I want you to all line up in front of us. You must say to me, "May I pet Cody?" I will say yes to some of you and no to others of you. If I say yes, you may pet him and go back to your seat. If I say no, you will go to the back of the line and come up again. Ask me again and I will say yes."

At the end of the Project, many of the children voted this experience as one of their favorites, after eighteen weeks of very hard work.

Lessons

've always been a staunch believer in the old adage that "In life, we always get the teachers we need." This applies not only to school settings, but to life in general.

One summer, on the last day of school, my home phone rang. I answered it and it was a neighbor on the other line "Nancy, Jimmy just got home with his sixth-grade teacher assignment and I am concerned. I understand that his teacher is not a good disciplinarian."

I knew Jimmy's family as neighbors and I said, "Oh, my goodness. He doesn't need strong discipline. I would let it go. "

Jimmy's dad was a very nice man, but he was old enough to be Jimmy's grandfather. At times, I had felt that he was a bit too stern with Jimmy. I didn't know his sixth-grade teacher very well, but I did know that he was very low-key

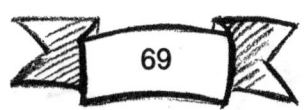

and very kind. I made it a practice to never comment on another teacher to a parent or to anyone else. It was not kind or professional.

Jimmy's sixth grade year came and went and, in the spring, his mother called me again near the end of the school-year.

"Nancy, I am so glad you gave me that advice last fall about Jimmy's teacher. Today, we had to have our dog put down and I wrote a note to Jimmy's teacher and asked him to 'keep an eye on Jimmy' today, in case he had a problem. Before Jimmy got home from school, his teacher called and said that Jimmy had been okay through the day. Jimmy and I both learned that men can be gentle, kind, and caring. Thank you so much."

My belief in the adage was made even stronger that day.

Father and Son

I n 1965, when I first arrived in Hershey, I had an un-usual combination of children. There were twenty-two boys and nine girls in my class. Thanks to my wonder-ful principal, I had some help from his support and sage advice. Some of the boys were a bit of a challenge, but I valued the challenge. I was determined to prove my two former principals wrong by their giving me unsatisfacto-ries' in my evaluations.

Thirty-one years later, at Back-to-School night, a young man walked into my room and gave me a hug. "Hi, Miss Miller," and identified himself. "I just told my son, when he got you for his teacher, 'You don't mess with this woman.'"

He was one of my original students. I don't remember ever having to chastise him for anything. The same was true with his child.

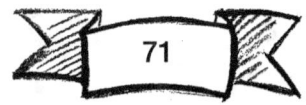

It humbles me to know that I taught two generations of children in my wonderful school.

From Helicopter to Snowplow

By the time I retired in 1996, we had endured about a decade of Helicopter Parents. They hovered over their children and their school environment. They tried to micromanage most of their child's experiences. I never had much of a problem with this issue because, by that time, I had had many years of teaching in that town. I had a reputation of being tough but kind, so they rarely questioned my authority. If there were a problem, we'd have a conference and resolve the issue to everyone's satisfaction.

Today, school personnel, from superintendent to custodian is faced with what are referred to as Snowplow Parents. The parent tries to clear the way for a child in every way. They try to choose their child's teacher, try to determine the class make-up, and even try to dictate

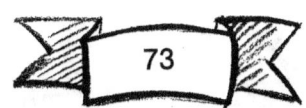

curriculum. They don't want the child to ever experience defeat, failure or any negative emotion. How will the child ever learn, that, many times failure in one experience leads to success in a new venture? How will the child ever learn to fend for himself/herself in life's challenges?

I was never a parent, but I mothered some two thousand children over thirty-seven years of teaching. I am very blessed that I had my career when I did. I respected the parents and they respected me. What a blessing.

Todd

I t shocks me that my first graders and my first fifth graders are one year apart and are in their mid-sixties! Most of them are probably retired.

I am a frequent visitor to the Ronald McDonald House in Hershey. Todd, one of my fifth graders, was the House Manager there for years. One day when I was there, he told me that he was about to retire at the end of the year. I told him that, after he retired, I would like to take him to lunch.

We met for lunch at a restaurant about halfway between Hershey and Carlisle, where I had moved a few years before. We had a wonderful time reminiscing and laughing like two old friends. After about two hours, we hugged and promised to keep in touch. To my delight, he said, "You know, I always felt safe and loved in your room." What more could a teacher ask of a beloved student!

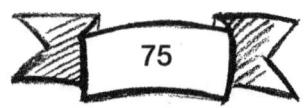

Addendum

On my way home, I was driving and suddenly, a local policeman stopped me. I always observe the speed limit and had never been stopped. I opened my window.

A young township officer said, "Have you been drinking?"

"Just coffee and water at lunch."

"Are you on drugs?"

"Just my prescriptions."

"Well, you were going 55 miles an hour in a 45-mile zone."

"Well, I am on a kind of high emotionally."

I told him a short version of what had happened and he laughed.

"Well, that's a new one. I never heard that one before. I'm going to give you only a warning, but be more careful next time."

"Thank you very much."

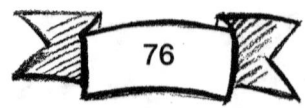

"I Didn't Say That"

She was our new principal and I could tell from the very outset that it was not a good thing! My teacher friends and I had gone in to school the week before it started to get our rooms ready. There were four or five of us standing at the intersection of our hall and the long hall that led to the Office – a good two blocks away! Stephanie strutted down the ramp toward us. When she got to us, she stopped and introduced herself and we did the same.

When I told her my name, she said, "Oh, you're the one who makes more money than I do." It was none of her business how much I made.

Point #1. I was older than she and had more experience than she!

Point #2. I had 61 credits beyond my Masters Degree! The credits were not in a program because I never wanted

to be an administrator. I wanted my own classroom and my own kids! I took courses in Children's Literature and other subjects which would broaden my horizons as a teacher. Our wonderful district paid for our courses in increments of 10, 20, 30, 45 credits beyond our Master' Degree. At each interval, our salary was raised permanently. Most of my credits were in reading instruction and library science. I didn't tell her because it was none of her business!

My room was the largest classroom in our building because it had been a Special Education room and the portable partition had been removed. When we had a meeting for fifth grade teachers, it was always held in my room.

One morning, Stephanie had a meeting in my room about "a wonderful new way to teach reading". I listened for as long as I could and said, "I think it's a 'crock of shit.' " My brother, later, said I should have stopped with 'Crock'. By that time in my career (probably twenty years). I'd had it with non-educators telling me how to teach my kids. I certainly wasn't perfect, but I knew a lot more about ten-year-olds than they did! I'd had it! As it turned out, my teacher friends felt and thought the same thing, but I was the big-mouth in the group.

Within a few days, I had a note to meet with our superintendent. I had been reported by Stephanie to have

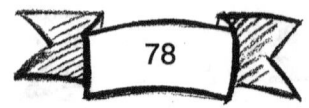

said, "You're full of _____." Now, I'm not stupid! I may have thought it, but I certainly didn't say it!

I met with the superintendent and told her what really had happened!

Within a week, Stephanie was gone!

I have a feeling that the incident was just "the straw that broke the camel's back."

Good riddance!

The Letter

13 Hendel Loop
Carlisle, PA 17015
August 15, 2020

Guiding Eyes for the Blind
611 Granite Springs Road
Yorktown Heights, NY 10598

Dear Mr. Panek,

I wanted to share a wonderful experience I had years ago at Guiding Eyes for the Blind. I have included it in a book I am writing about my wonderful career. It is called "A Very High Calling," which I feel my lifetime work was for me. I taught fifth grade in Hershey, PA for thirty-one years and conversational English in high school in Poland for two years. As I typed your surname, I wondered if you might be Polish American.

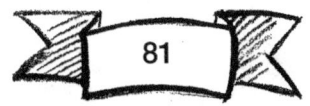

I am not sure about the name of the guide dog, but I think Kansas was his name. It gives me great pleasure to share it with you.

Sincerely,

Nancy Miller

Nancy Miller

He Needs More Training

was on sabbatical leave from my fifth-grade teaching job for the 1989-1990 school year. I wanted to expand my wonderful Helen Keller Project, an intensive, one semester project which encompassed my whole-language curriculum for eighteen weeks.

One of the major highlights of that year was my trip to Guiding Eyes for the Blind in Yorktown Heights, New York. I was there for a graduation ceremony, at which time the dog guides and their new masters/mistresses graduated after weeks of intensive training. There had been a picnic for the puppy raisers, dogs and new owners prior to the ceremony. The puppy raisers had been given beautiful color portraits of their grown puppy and its new owner.

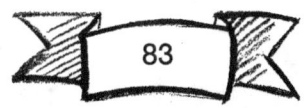

At some point in the ceremony a dog and his master were called to the front to receive their certificate. About halfway up the aisle, Kansas was distracted either by the sight or the scent of his puppy raisers and darted off to the right to see them. Fortunately, his master was steady enough on his feet that he didn't fall. The moderator, laughed and said, "Well, it is obvious that Kansas needs a few more days of training before we can let him go."

Ivy Green

I n 1989-1990, while on sabbatical leave from my job. I traveled to Ivy Green, Helen Keller's home in Tuscumbia, Alabama. There, I met Patty Johnson, Helen's niece. Her mother, Helen's younger sister, was the baby in the cradle in the scene in "The Miracle Worker" whom Helen pushed over in one of her frequent tantrums. Patty was post - middle age at this point and had a lovely home nearby. She was very friendly and gracious. She invited me and my friend for lunch in her home.

As we were finishing our lunch she said, "You know, you're eating your dessert with Annie Sullivan's silverware!"

I laughed and said, "Well, you'd better count it before I leave." We had a good laugh. We kept in touch for years after my visit.

Helen graduated from Radcliffe College with high honors and I always felt that Annie should have gotten the

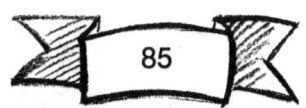

same honors – after all – she did at least as much work as Helen had done!

Bela

Bela had had a dysfunctional early childhood. Her father was in the Merchant Marines and the family lived in a California commune in the eighties. At two-and-a-half, she had repeatedly tried to feed her dead mother her breakfast. Her mother had overdosed and had been dead for a few days.

Her father had moved her home to Pennsylvania where his mother could help in raising her. I had her in fifth grade and she was a nice child. She was a tall natural blonde and was mild-mannered. It took a long time to find out about her history. Her dad was involved in her life and her grandmother was kind, but was too old and too old-fashioned to be very effective in guiding a ten-year-old girl.

At the end of fifth grade at a parent conference, I told her father that I would like to do some fun things with

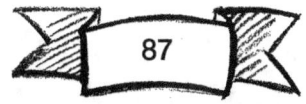

her over the summer. He thought that was a good idea. I had a friend who had a niece and nephew about her age and we could do things together. Throughout the summer, the five of us visited a local amusement park, visited a local cavern and took some rides to nearby parks and took picnic lunches with us. It was a nice summer. At the end of the summer, she and I went shopping for back-to-school clothes and supplies. One day when we were shipping for clothes, I was walking with her and we were looking at some clothing for her. I was behind her and giving my input. She turned around and said, somewhat pointedly, "Please don't hover."

I laughed and said, "Oh, Honey. That's how girls shop." The poor child didn't have a clue. When her dad took her shopping, he sat impatiently and wondered what had taken her so long. When her grandma took her, she disapproved of everything Bela liked.

Time passed and we saw each other often. We had dinner out and shopped many times. Occasionally, we got together with my friend and her niece and nephew.

When Bela was in eighth grade, it was announced that we would be in school until June 25, due to many snow days that winter. Bela was staying with me while her grandmother was in the hospital for an extended time. The

eighth graders had gone out on strike one day at lunch-time. I didn't know it until I got home about four o'clock.

Bela was sitting on the living room couch when I walked in the house, which was unusual. I looked into the living room and she said, "I made an error in judgment today. My friends went out on strike today when we found out how long we have to go this summer and I went with them. We got three days of out of school suspension."

"Did Beth go out?"

"No, because she knew she'd have consequences."

"Well, if you think you won't have consequences, you can think again."

"Well, we were just exercising our First Amendment rights."

"What do you know about the First Amendment?"

"Nothing."

"Well, that's going to be a part of your consequences. You will do research about that and give me a written report on it. Of course, that was before ready access to the internet.

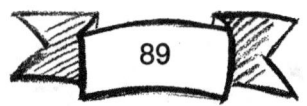

89

"You will spend time in the library and find out about the First Amendment."

I went to school the next day and talked with my wonderful principal. I told her that I was concerned about Bela being at home alone with some of her friend's 'on the loose.' The students were not to be on school grounds for those three days. Putting her job on the line, she gave me permission to have Bela in a small room attached to mine, with permission only to leave the room to use the bathroom. I carried her lunch to her from our cafeteria. After school, she went to the town library to do her research.

For the six weeks she was with me, she did her homework and did well on her quizzes and tests because she was bright. She had never done well because she hadn't applied herself. After she moved back with her grandmother, we often did things together. I would ask her how she was doing in school and was she doing her homework. The answer to both questions was no. I would ask her why and she would say, "Because no one cares."

"I care and you should too."

"My dad and my grandma don't care, so why should I?'

Four years later, she graduated and enlisted in the Navy.

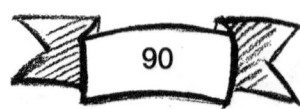

She was trained as a pastry chef and, no surprise to me, she graduated at the head of her class. I think of her often and have tried to find her, but to no avail.

I Earned It!

The year before I retired from my beloved calling, in 1996, I had a spring parent conference with Wendy. I had had three of her children and we were on a first-name basis. At the end of our conference, she said, "Nancy, do you know what the fourth graders call you?"

"No, tell me."

"Oh, I'd better not. It might hurt your feelings."

"Come on, Tell me."

"They call you Killer Miller."

"Oh, thank you. I really worked hard for that reputation.!"

Imagine! Thirty-one years before that afternoon, I was in serious danger of never being allowed to teach again-because

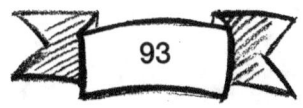

I wasn't good at classroom management! I am eternally grateful to Mr. Sterling King, my principal and Dr. L. Eugene Jacques, my superintendent for being willing to take a chance on me and guiding me so kindly. Truly, A VERY HIGH CALLING!

David

For a few years, I was an usher at the beautiful Hershey Theater. As I remember, we weren't paid much, but we stayed to see many wonderful plays and/or concerts. Many famous plays with famous people in the casts -many national touring companies!

One Saturday night, I had the good fortune of ushering for a performance of Les Misérables. After finding a seat, I glanced at the Playbill. In the listing under the "ensemble" heading, I recognized the name of one of my former "kids". He was a young man by now, but I could pick him out of the crowd in the small group of about twenty.

After the play, I found my way backstage to see him. I got a big hug and he said, "Tomorrow, I will be Jean Val Jean," (the main character) "because I am the understudy and the guy who played him tonight is not well enough to do it tomorrow afternoon."

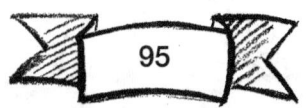

"I'll be here! I'll probably be late, but I'll be here!"

On Sunday, after church and dinner in Carlisle, I got to the theatre in time to hear David sing "Bring Him Home". What a voice!

Back stage, I said, "I didn't know in fifth grade that you had a nice voice."

"Neither did I." But, in high school, Mr. Hartman "discovered" me and I was in "Brigadoon."

We had a nice hug and I have a few of his CDs.

The last I heard of him, a few years back, he and his family are living in Lancaster, PA and he is a choral director at a large church.

Elizabeth

Recently, I was attending a dear friend's memorial "Celebration of Life" event. Family and friends were milling about in the backyard on a beautiful early summer day. There were tears and laughter in the group, sharing memories of our much-loved mother and friend.

I was standing on the edge of the pool and a woman came up to me. I knew that I should have recognized her, but she readily identified herself as the mother of one of my former fifth graders.

"You're Nancy Miller, aren't you?"

"Yes, I am."

"Well. My daughter Elizabeth had you in fifth grade and she loved you." She is now in her early fifties and she still talks about her Helen Keller Project you did with the children.

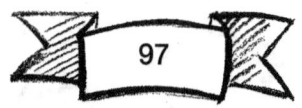

It was so wonderful. It taught them to respect people with handicaps. It was a great whole-language experience, and it taught them so many important life skills. When she was still a child and we'd watch a movie together at home, she'd say, 'That's an example of comic relief' or if we would get emotional over some incident in the film, she'd say, 'That's called empathy.' It was such a wonderful learning experience. It taught the children so many important things."

I took her hand and thanked her. For me, it changed what started out as a sad day into what it was meant to be "A Celebration of Life."

Christie

Christie was my next-door neighbor and we were both thrilled when she ended up in my English class. Like all my English students, she learned her 45 prepositions in alphabetical order. She was an excellent student and a very nice little girl. Years passed and I moved away.

About forty years passed and I was back in Hershey for lunch with friends. Christie was there with a friend. As she was leaving, she spotted me in a nearby booth and came over to me and gave me a hug. "I know you said may years ago, "No one will stop you on Chocolate Avenue and ask you to say your prepositions in alphabetical order," but here we are at the Chocolate Avenue Grille, and I can still say them, but I don't have time right now. Gotta get back to work.'

A few minutes later, I walked out onto the parking lot and she was backing out of her parking space. She and her

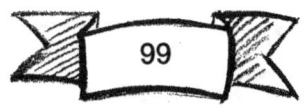

friend were laughing. I walked over to her car and said, "What's so funny?"

"I just said them all for her and she thinks it's so funny, after all these years." I got another hug and we each headed on our way. The long-term rewards for a teacher!

So Blessed

was back in Hershey to meet with teacher-friends for lunch. About an hour before that date, I did a bit of grocery shopping. Less than twenty feet into the store, I met up with one of my fifth-graders, now at least fifty years old. We had a few laughs, shared a warm hug and moved on to do our shopping. Less than ten minutes later, in the pastry department in the back of the store, a woman, coming toward me said, with a broad smile on her face said, "You haven't changed. I'd know you anywhere!" I smiled and said, "You have to help me." She identified herself and I instantly remembered her. I'd had her and three of her four sisters in fifth grade and the family had been neighbors for fifteen years in her youth. We chatted and "caught up" with each other for about fifteen minutes. I proceeded to the front of the store to check out.

In the parking lot, I was putting my few groceries in the back of the car and someone tapped me on the shoulder. I

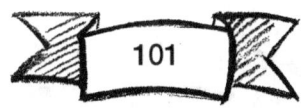

turned around and a woman about fifty said, "About, above, across, after, against, along, among, around, at…"

We both had broad smiles on our faces and I said, "You'll have to help me." She told me her name and said, "you had me and my brother Joe in fifth grade. You told us that no one would ever stop us on Chocolate Avenue and ask us to recite our prepositions in alphabetical order, but I can still say them, and so can Joe. We learned so much from you and we love you."

Thank you so much," I said with a lump in my throat. After a wonderful hug, I got in my car and had a good gratitude cry.

Truly a High Calling through all those Years!

Madison

S he was tall and mature-looking for a twelve-year-old. She was our oldest child in our summer day-camp for kids. We kidded her about "aging out" because her birthday was the week before the end of our program. We'd laugh and tell her she couldn't come back after her birthday, and she'd laugh, knowing we were teasing. She was very creative and often would talk about her artwork at home. One day she told us that she would soon run out of space in her bedroom and would have to start using the ceiling as display space.

One day, the lesson was about classical music. The teacher for the week and the director of our program came in with instruments. She had a violin and he had a clarinet. After a lesson on music, they challenged the children to see if they could name the tune they were about to play. They started and Madison jumped up and waved her hand wildly.

"I know that! It's Beethoven's Ninth Symphony!" The rest of the children didn't have a clue. The teacher started to say, "No, it's…' and she looked at the music. "You're right!" The title at the very top was "Ode to Joy," but on the right just above the score, it read "Beethoven's Ninth Symphony."

We adults in the room clapped and the children followed. At that moment, Madison was ten feet tall!

Part Three
Poland

Wabinska

It was my second year of teaching high school conversational English in Poland. I was really excited about returning after two years at home back in Pennsylvania. I'd had such a beautiful experience my first year in the beautiful Polish town of Strzelce Opolskie.

About a month before I left for Poland, my new mentor, Marysia Wabinska, called me and told me not to expect to ever be invited to her home while I was in Poland. This was in very sharp contrast to my mentor teacher in Strzelce, also Marysia. There, I instantly became a part of her small family. They even had a Thanksgiving celebration for me
I helped them in their beautiful allotment garden all year and they kept me in full supply of fresh vegetables all winter from the cold cellar.

I arrived and met Marysia and things seemed okay, but somewhat cold. She told me what my duties were; primarily,

to get the seniors ready for their English Matury – an oral and written test they must pass in three languages in order to graduate. As an English teacher with 31 years of experience, I knew how to teach it! She wanted me to take the 75 possible Matury questions and have the kids get up and answer them – random questions – at which time I might hear from three – maybe four – students in a class period. The other twenty were supposed to pay attention!

On the other hand, I wanted to teach them common suffixes and prefixes I had taught in fifth grade. They could make hundreds of words with these by adding them to a root word. One day, I asked them to make up as many words as they could using the root word "tie" and the suffixes and prefixes they had learned. The class came up with 23 new words with those word parts. The kids were amazed. I had heard from every kid in the class instead of just three or four. When Marysia found out, she approached me and told me that I wasn't doing what I came there to do. I told her the African story about the man who taught his tribesmen to fish so they would eat for a lifetime instead of giving them a fish for one meal. She didn't like that.

I had taken abut one hundred beautiful colored magazine pictures and photos of beautiful scenes in America. I fanned them out in my hands and the kids came up, chose one at random and talked about it for about two minutes.

I asked questions and the kids answered them. I corrected his/her pronunciation and sentence structure. They were very open to kind, constructive criticism and felt good about themselves.

When Marysia found out that I was doing it my way, she told the kids that my class wasn't important. I didn't give grades, but I always gave my input to the English teacher so it could be part of their English grade. She even told the parents, who were paying for their kids to come to me, that I wasn't doing my job. After that, some of the kids started to skip class.

About once a month, there was a meeting after school and the teachers got up and told the rest of the faculty what they did in their classroom. It was in Polish, of course, so I didn't usually attend because that was the total agenda and I don't understand Polish. When I was aware of this, I asked my dear friend Basia to help me to tell the group what I do in class, because Marysia had also told the faculty that I was not doing my job.

I dictated what I did in class and she transcribed it and read it to the group at the next meeting which I attended. Afterwards, a lot of the teachers and the head mistress (principal) came up to me and apologized for how I had been treated. I made a lot of new friends that day!

Apparently, I was the only native speaker from America which that school had had. The others had been from England and Australia, and of course, spoke British English. That is what the kids learned, but they preferred American English, for it is much less complicated. Others who had gone before me were not teachers of English. They were very qualified to teach conversational English, but they had taught art, gym, and history.

When I think about that whole experience, I think that Marysia felt threatened by me. The kids loved me and they didn't like her. My classes were fun and non-threatening. She did not have a good reputation as a nice person and the kids knew it. The kids had fun in my class and they LEARNED English – practical things they could use. They felt better prepared to take their scary orals in English because of the things we had done in our class.

I certainly don't regret that experience because I was in my beloved Poland again. I traveled every weekend and met a lot of wonderful people. I saw my wonderful Polish friends from my first year there, and got to travel to new places all over Europe. I learned how to happily co-exist with someone who didn't like me or respect me. I learned a lot of valuable lessons-lessons that I have put to good use since then.

Naivete'

For all of my thirty-four years of teaching in Pennsylvania, I thought that children should not start kindergarten until they were six years old – especially the boys who mature more slowly than the girls. I always jokingly said my fifth graders were all ten chronologically, but the boys were eight and the girls were thirteen.

Then I retired and taught in Poland for two years, where they start school at seven. What an eye-opener!

I was a native speaker in high school and taught conversational English. The students had to have four years of British English to graduate. It was my job to have the kids speak, learn vocabulary and be comfortable using English. We had a wonderful time. We played games, sang and conversed. I did not know British English. The kids wanted to speak American English. They already knew a lot of American English from watching American television for years.

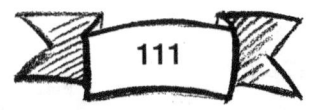

I never made written assignments for the kids, but they knew they could write anything out for themselves if I made an assignment for the next week.

One day in the spring, I made an assignment for the next week in my senior classes. The girls were to think about what they would like to find in a husband and the boys were to do the same in looking for a wife.

The girls said that they would like to marry a man who was kind, well-educated and it wouldn't hurt if he were good-looking.

The first few boys had taken the assignment seriously and said about the same things as the girls had said.

One young man got up and said, "She has to be blonde and have big boobs." We all laughed and the rest of the boys repeated what he had said.

It was then that I realize that if a boy starts school at seven, he graduates at nineteen or twenty! A nineteen-year-old man has no business in high school!

Mateusz (Matthew)

On Mondays, when I was teaching in Poland, I would ask my high school English students to tell me what they had done over the weekend.

Mateusz raised his hand and said, in good English, "I was in Warsaw and I saw my first nigger."

"Oh, Honey, you can't say it like that." My students had learned a lot of their English by watching a lot of British and American television.

I proceeded to give the kids a brief history of the proper terms to use.

"When I was growing up in the 1940's and 50's they were called negroes. Through the 60's and 70's we referred to them as 'colored' and in the 80's and 90's, we call them blacks." This was in the 1996-97 school rear.

Mateusz looked at me and said, "Thank you so much."

Lukasz (Luke)

My second year of teaching in Poland was in a small town near the beautiful city of Wroclaw about 100 kilometers east of the German border. During World War II, it was known as Breslau. I was teaching conversational English to high school students who were taught The King's English by their Polish teachers. It was my job to make the kids comfortable speaking English. Of course, they wanted to speak American English since they had grown up with American television, (and some British television). They preferred American because it was much less complicated. We played a lot of word games, sang simple songs, and each student had to get up each period and speak. It was my job to correct any mistakes and they were very open to kind, constructive criticism.

Each class had about 15 kids in it and our room was a small one on a mezzanine around the auditorium. We were not near any other classrooms, so we could make as much

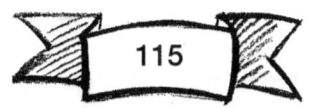

noise as we wanted. One day, as I was approaching the room, I saw a few of the girls sitting in the hallway and said it was time to come to class. When I started class, I had only about seven students – all boys. Some of the girls had an attitude, so I went on with class.

We had such a good time that day talking about their favorite television shows and movies. We laughed and enjoyed the class so much.

When they were leaving the room, Lukasz turned at the door and said, "You're different from our other teachers.

"How's that?"

"You like us."

I thought "How sad." I had also experienced some of that reaction to some of their teachers. Some of them were there only because it was their job. It was certainly very different from my first experience in Strzelce, two years earlier.

Krakow

As was my Monday custom in Strzelce, I asked the kids what they had done over the weekend. One of the kids asked me what I had done.

"I spent the weekend in Krakow." The kids laughed. I must have looked confused. The same kid said, "That's not way we say it. Krakow has an accent mark over the o which makes it a double o and the w is pronounced like a v. So, it is pronounced Krakoof." We all had a good laugh and I thanked him.

Agata (Agatha)

It was cold, snowy evening in Strzelce, Poland. I was teaching conversational English in that beautiful town in south-central Poland in the region of Silesia. I did some private tutoring with some of my high school students. Agata was one of my most serious students. She was getting ready to go across the parking lot to her flat. As she was putting her boots on, she said, "There's one word I don't understand in English. I was hoping it would be in American English and not in "The King's English."

"What's that, Honey?"

"Well, I hear it quite a lot. It's the word firstavull."

"Do you mean festival? Put it in a sentence."

"No, I know festival. Firstavull, we did this, then we did that."

"Oh, you mean First of all."

"Oh, of course. Now I know. Thanks so much."

She went on to college and majored in English. She is now teaching in her hometown and is the head of the English department in her alma mater.

Michal

After teaching conversational English in high school in Poland I had the wonderful opportunity to host young Polish "kids" who were serving a four-month business internship in Central Pennsylvania businesses This was the other arm of Pennsylvania Partnerships Abroad, the foundation which had sponsored my teaching in Poland. They were about twenty-three years old and were in college, studying for their Masters of Business administration degree from a university in my favorite Polish city of Wroclaw.

In the fall of 2000, Michal (Mike) was one of about twenty young students to arrive in Pennsylvania. He was tall and a lot of my friends thought he looked like Tom Cruise. It was love at first sight for me. He was smart, kind and good looking and had a funny sense of humor.

His job was in nearby Harrisburg and I took him there every morning and picked him up in the late afternoon.

One day I picked him up and said, "I'm meeting some friends for dinner. You're welcome to join us, or we can pick something up for you, or you can make something at home." I knew what he would say.

"I'd like to join you if that's okay. I was excited. He was very social and I was pleased because I had told my friends a lot about him and they would be pleased to finally meet him.

I'm glad that I asked him what he would order, because his answer was, "I'm going to order a booger." The Polish roll their r's and our words with and "r" in the middle are difficult for them. They have a hard time with our word "rural." I realized that this was a teachable moment for us.

I laughed and said, "No, Honey. You can't order a booger. Make your mouth like a fish and say 'bur-ger' slowly. The rest of the way to the restaurant, Mike said 'bur-ger.'

Twenty years later, we still laugh about it!

In the fall of 2018, I got an email from Mike and he asked if I would tutor his seven-year-old daughter Kornelia in English. Of course, I said I'd love to. In Poland, they are now teaching English in primary school. For

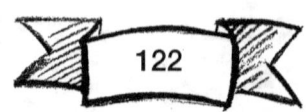

about a year, on Sunday mornings at 8:00 my time, (2PM Polish time) Kornelia and I had a fun lesson for about a half an hour.

Over eleven years, from 2000 on, I had the pleasure of hosting eleven young Polish students in my home and in my heart.

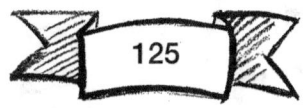

The Pantry

I was home from teaching my first year in Poland and was out for lunch with friends at a local restaurant called The Pantry. A woman came up to our table and introduced herself. I had had both of her children in school. She said, "I understand that you taught in Poland last year. I am teaching fifth grade in a local Christian school. I'd love for you to come and tell my children about Poland."

"I'd love to. I'll need at least two long tables for my alphabet display and my artifacts." Her reply was, "No problem. But you can't mention the Catholic church."

"Well, you can't give a talk about Poland without talking about the Catholic church. It is probably the country in Europe which has been taken over more times by hostile neighbors and their faith kept them strong. And, Pope John Paul II was the first non-Italian pope in history – from 1978-2005!"

She said, "Well, I'll call you about scheduling a time."

I was so stunned; I didn't know what to say. I knew I couldn't do that! I went home and prayed about it and called my pastor. We talked and prayed about it.

She called and we set a date. I told her my concern and she repeated her wishes. I reminded her about how, in 1989, President Reagan, Pope John Paul and Lech Walesa abolished the Soviet Union. She was not impressed. I told her that I had to do what I had to do.

I took all my things and met with her children. They were very attentive and things went well. When I got to their history and their strength as a people, I told the children, that strong faith kept the people strong.

She jerked in her chair. Oh, well. I did what I felt was the right thing to do. She didn't invite me back – and that's okay.

A Family Affair

I lived in a wonderful retirement community for eight years after moving back to Carlisle and a friend of many years also lived here. During my thirty-one years of teaching in Hershey, Dina was our school nurse for a number of those years. We have become good friends.

Dina was widowed as a young woman and raised her five children alone for many years. Later, she married a man who was raising his three young children alone. They married and blended their two families. In the ensuing years, I taught three of Dina's children and all three of Bill's children in fifth grade.

This past Christmas season, I was walking the long hallway leading to our dining room in our community center. I saw a sign on the door of our card room which said that the room was reserved for Dina's family for a party, on a night later in the week. I saw her in the dining room a few minutes later and asked her if I could "crash" her party. She said, "Of course."

I had not seen some of them since they had become adults, but I think I would have known some of them anywhere. They didn't know I was coming, so when I popped into the room, there were some surprised faces.

The next hour was filled with laughter and silliness. They told funny stories about me and I returned the favor! It was so much fun! They told stories about classroom happenings, some of which I remembered, some I didn't. I told of funny thing which happened between any one of them and me. Like the kids today would say, we had fun "bustin" on each other.

I left with such a wonderful feeling of having had a valuable relationship with Dina's loving family.

Afterword
Full Circle

I sincerely hope and pray that, from my wonderful 37 years of teaching, I have come full circle. I hope that I have taught my children wonderful and valuable lessons – well beyond their English lessons. I hope I taught them to be kind and to treat others as they would like to be treated and to pay that forward.

We are all God's children and should be treated with love and respect. We are all sisters and brothers in God's holy family.

www.ingramcontent.com/pod-product-compliance
Lightning Source LLC
Chambersburg PA
CBHW071004120626
46546CB00003B/927